WHAT DO YOU FEEL?

Simple thoughts of a single Christian

Joseph Olabiyi Johnson

Visit us online at <u>www.authorsonline.co.uk</u>

Ideal theme song for this book is:
'To Da River' by T-Bone, Zane & Montell Jordan

CHRISTIANITY 101

CONTENTS

INTRODUCTION

My name is Joseph Olabiyi Johnson and I would like to share the thoughts that have gone through my mind since I gave my life to Christ in 2003.

Now as you read through my thoughts, please bear in mind that I'm not claiming to be any kind of expert or even impose any kind of doctrine on anyone. All I'm doing is displaying my perspective of things around me.

My advice to anyone reading this book is to take my views and compare them to his/her own and then think. Who knows? You might learn something.

Enjoy....

THE TRUE STRUCTURE OF CHRISTIANITY

The term 'structure' on a very basic level can be defined as an orderly system of interrelated parts. 'Parts' here could be taken literally or could represent procedures, hierarchy, or a set of formulas.

Anything that can carry out any task efficiently has some kind of structure, be it a huge company, the human body or a blender. Companies that go bankrupt or fail to reach their targets have a tarnished or unsuitable structure of some kind. If the structure of the human body is negatively tampered with it becomes sick, and if your blender stops working it is because one of its parts is no longer inter-related to the others.

Now Christianity from my point of view can be defined as the quest for spiritual growth undertaken by following the teachings of Jesus Christ aka the Son of God. And Christianity, like everything else, isn't exempt from the need for structure.

Now when many people hear the term 'Structure within Christianity' the first thing that would probably come into their heads is the hierarchy or departmental structure within a Church building. This is understandable seeing as a <u>true</u> house of God should nurture the spiritual growth of all its members. However, the foundation of every Church building starts with its members, which means the true structure of Christianity begins with the structure of the individual Christian.

1 John 4 verse 16
'God is love, and he who abides in love abides in God, and God in him.'

The true structure of Christianity is love. Now many people might ask, 'What's love got to do with it?' Well the entire teachings of Jesus Christ are rooted in love, and if examined you would find that billions of people without hesitation would admit that love is the most powerful and most needed force ever to exist.

For any individual Christian to have a strong structure he/she must:

1. Love God
2. Love one's self
3. Love the people around them

1. <u>LOVE GOD</u> – Loving God is not as hard as many may think, in fact it is very similar to loving a fellow human being. First you start by getting to know God through study of the Bible and listening to sermons when attending a church or watching Christian TV, or listening to sermons recorded on tape or CD.

Talking to God a lot through prayer is also a good way to get closer to him. Now when I say prayer, I don't mean a religious or ceremonial act, because despite what many may think or say true Christianity isn't a religion. You could pray in literally any way you feel comfortable: some people pray in their heads, some pray out loud, some pray while they walk, some pray while they watch TV and even while playing video games.

And talking to God doesn't always have to be about asking for some kind of favour since you could literally confide in him about your day or even ask him how he is. Prayer was very daunting for me as I prayed in a ceremonial and religious manner, which often led to boredom, but when I got the above revelation, I literally began to pray at any time and anywhere. Praying in tongues is also a great way to talk to God because it is simply praying with your heart with a total disregard for language.

2. <u>LOVE ONE'S SELF</u> – Loving one's self is something many people are unable to do. Loving yourself has a lot to do with celebrating who you are and not being ashamed or discontent with any aspect of your identity. A lot of people think that being a Christian means giving up an element of one's personality and becoming <u>holier than thou</u>; which is basically indulging in a fantasy world that God didn't orchestrate. Becoming a Christian essentially entails eliminating your bad habits only and allocating your talents to positive endeavours. This would usually mean one's checking himself/herself mentally, physically, and spiritually.

3. <u>LOVE THE PEOPLE AROUND YOU</u> – Loving the people around you doesn't mean being lovey-dovey with everyone you meet or know (if you can then that will be a bonus), however it does mean:

- Not keeping any kind of grudge against anyone.
- Not wishing evil upon anyone, including those who offend you.
- Going out of your way to help anyone you can, even if it is with a prayer.
- Greeting as many people with a smile as you possibly can because a smile in itself can go a long way.

- Being prepared to offer sincere friendship.

Anyone that does not live by this structure will find it very difficult to find complete happiness and contentment in this life and even in the next.

SHORT STORY 1

REDEDICATING MY LIFE TO CHRIST IN 2003

After re-dedicating my life to Christ in 2003, I immediately made a conscious effort to eliminate bad habits in my life, most of which a lot of the world would not consider a big deal. These habits included smoking, drinking and casual sex.

Then, as I began to further embrace my new life, I came to realise that spiritual growth as a born-again Christian went far beyond counting good deeds and habits. The essence of true spiritual growth as a Christian, I found, dwelt in the process of refusing to have a tainted heart or possessing negative thinking patterns. For me this meant facing the fact that fundamentally I was a very proud and temperamental person. These were traits that often led to my telling lies and harbouring a judgemental spirit.

Embracing the life of a born-again Christian has also made me realise the spiritual, mental and physical futility of holding absolutely any grudges against any individual. After coming to this realisation, I made a conscious effort to make peace with everyone that hurt me or perhaps I had hurt. This allowed me to create a closer relationship with my family and to open up the possibility of renewed friendships.

I've also developed a sincere and personal relationship with God that has made me realise that although I'm not perfect, striving for perfection is a good start.

Romans 3 verse 23
'For all have sinned and have fallen short of the glory of God'

My personal relationship with God has also taught me not to be discouraged as a Christian, even when I make mistakes, or find myself giving into sin. (However I don't see this as a licence to consciously take advantage of God's mercy).

Philippians 3 verse 13
'Brethren, I do not count myself to have apprehended, but one thing I do forgetting those things which are behind and reaching forward to those things, which are ahead.'

The most important lesson I've learnt so far as a born-again Christian is that true spiritual growth can only come when you stay true to God and yourself. A Pastor reiterated this in one of his sermons by saying:

'True integrity isn't what people think of you, but what God thinks of you.'

The most important change that has taken place in me is coming to the realisation that when you claim to be a born-again Christian and then choose not to walk in the path of holiness, you are not deceiving the people around you and you're certainly not deceiving God; you are simply deceiving yourself.

Despite all these changes that have taken place in me so far, there is still much for me to learn.

POEM 1

WHAT IS REAL LOVE?

Real love makes people feel comfortable
Real love makes people feel free
Real love makes people feel happy
Real love makes people feel sad
Real love makes people feel guilty
Real love makes people feel angry
Real love speaks with sincere actions
Real love never relies only on sincere words
Real love helps people discover who they really are
In truth real love from a human being can go only so far
Real love isn't self-centred and with your heart it wouldn't
play
Real love would at least make the effort to meet you half
away
Real love is straightforward
Real love will leave you with the truth
Real love will accept the fact you're not perfect
Real love will always keep you in the loop
If you have really loved someone
And all they can do is keep you at bay
Then real love should make you
Walk away.

BEING BORN AGAIN?

The term 'born-again Christian' is being used now mainly because the term 'Christian' by itself has been tarnished. Many people just adopt the title 'Christian' once they go to church or once they are born into a Christian family. The term born-again Christian simply represents the individual that has made a conscious decision to accept Jesus Christ as his or her Lord and personal saviour.

Giving one's life to Christ is like the beginning of a journey of self-improvement through the teachings of Jesus Christ. Once an individual gives his or her life to Christ, improvements start to manifest themselves physically, mentally and of course spiritually.

In John 3 verses 3–6, Jesus Christ states that for anyone to see the kingdom of God it is vital that he/she becomes a born-again Christian. Now like I said earlier, becoming a born-again Christian is the beginning of a journey. However, many feel it is a race to see who can do the most good deeds before they die, which is a very serious misconception.

It is written in the Bible (Isaiah 64 verse 6) that a man's righteousness to God is nothing more than filthy rags. This basically means that if an ordinary person did a million good deeds per second, it cannot guarantee God's approval.

What many people fail to realise is that Jesus Christ is the ticket into heaven and once you accept him as your Lord and personal saviour, salvation and holiness is given to you freely. After this, you have to make a conscious effort to walk in the path of holiness.

Being issued with free salvation and holiness is like being issued with a free new car. Just because you received it freely doesn't mean you shouldn't spend money on maintaining it. Today, many people are holy but they haven't begun to walk in the path of holiness; meaning that they made up their minds to be bornagain, but have refused to give up habits that tarnish them in one way or the other.

Being a born-again Christian is about changing the heart from a selfish one into a selfless one and not trying to come across as holier than thou so that people around you will sing your praises.

Giving your life to Christ not only helps you to stay true to God and yourself, but it will also keep all areas of your life in check. In most cases, the transition may seem hard but becoming a born-again Christian is actually the best decision one could make.

WHAT IS SPIRITUAL GROWTH?

As a born-again Christian, spiritual growth is simply getting to know God and understanding him more and then applying this understanding in your everyday life. So, for instance, we just learnt that sucking up to God is futile. So applying that new piece of understanding would mean aiming to serve and praise God with a genuine heart.

Growing spiritually brings us closer to God and could bring us to a stage where we get advice directly from the Almighty himself. And there are really only two things that stand in our way of getting to this stage; they are Laziness and Iniquity.

Now the Bible says that we are Sinners and have fallen short of the glory of God. However, if an individual consciously commits Sin (Iniquity) and does absolutely nothing about it, spiritual growth simply won't happen.

Now to grow spiritually as a Christian, one should start by going to a Church gathering. A good way to get to know God is by visiting him in his home.

Then pick up the habit of studying the Bible for this is a good way of seeing God's attitude in words.

And the third and most effective way of growing spiritually is by simply surrounding one's self with like-minded Christians and a good way of doing this is by making friends with them or getting more active within a Church gathering.

Spiritual growth is essential for anyone who wants to attain inner and outer prosperity within this life and the next.

SHORT STORY 2

THE HOLY SPIRIT AND ME

John 14 verse 17
'The spirit of truth whom the world cannot receive, because it neither sees him or knows him; but you know him, for he dwells with you and will be in you.'

While rededicating my life to Christ, I was told that the Holy Spirit is part of God, very influential and powerful, has emotions, will and mind, and convicts us of sin.

Even though on a logical level I was able to understand the words put to me, I was still unable to comprehend their true meanings and ended up labelling the Holy Spirit as nothing more than the Christian term for a conscience. But as my relationship with God developed, I found he was much more than that.

My first major encounter with the Holy Spirit after rededicating my life to Christ came after I had an argument with a close friend. Even now when I break down what happened on a logical level, I feel like I had every right to end the friendship and move on with my life. But the Holy Spirit not only convicted me to forgive my friend, but it also convicted me to apologise for not being a more understanding friend myself. And it did this through thoughts, people and music.

Eventually, I listened to the Holy Spirit and now my friend and I are closer than ever for we now truly understand each other, which is a miracle considering that at one point, I was almost certain that our friendship was over.

The Holy Spirit is another arm of God, which he uses regularly to communicate with us.

POEM 2

POEM FOR A FRIEND

She's one in a million
A very special person
Bright, beautiful and smart
An angel in my eyes
Right from the very start
Fate may seem cruel
By putting me in an arm of another
But angel remember one thing
Girlfriends come and go
But true love and friendship last forever

THE MOST IMPORTANT ASPECT OF BEING A CHRISTIAN

What many people fail to realise is that Christianity isn't a religion, because religion is about what you can do for your God while Christianity is really about what your God can do for you. This is why, fundamentally, God isn't really moved by whether a man prays 1000 times a day or whether he fasts 365 times a year.

Christianity being God's search for man is displayed in the Bible when, through her own doing, Hagar found herself alone and pregnant in the desert. She didn't go down on her knees to pray, but an angel of God still found her and guided her onto the right path. This shows that God is constantly looking for opportunities to show us his love.

However, despite the above truth, many individuals either on a conscious or subconscious level believe God is interested in what they can do for him. Praying is good, going to a Church gathering is good, preaching the Gospel is good and performing miracles in the name of Jesus Christ is good. But all the above would be deemed worthless in the eyes of God if done with the wrong heart.

Matthew 7 verse 22–23
'Many will say to me in that day, "Lord, Lord, have we not prophesised in your name, cast out demons in your name, and done many wonders in your name?" And then I will declare to them, "I never knew you; depart from me, you who practice lawlessness!"'

The most important aspect of any Christian is his/her heart because the human heart in its natural form is desperately wicked as pointed out in Jeremiah 17 verse 9. This is why

Christians need to go out of their way to positively condition their hearts.

A positively conditioned heart is something all Christians should aim to have or strive towards because it helps breed a level of faith that can only be classed as extra-ordinary. Abraham displayed this faith when he was ready to sacrifice his only son, Isaac, in Genesis chapter 22.

A positively conditioned heart also breeds spiritual stamina, which will enable a Christian to stay true to God and him/herself even in the most difficult times. Jesus Christ displayed this kind of stamina by forgiving his crucifiers while nailed on the cross.

Luke 23 verse 34
'Then Jesus said, "Father, forgive them, for they do not know what they do."'

There are four ideal steps to positively shaping one's heart and the first one is asking God to help make it happen through prayer. The second step involves studying the word of God. The third step involves an individual being extremely honest with him/herself. While the fourth step involves an individual frequently questioning his/her own motives when carrying out any act – especially if it is in the name of our Heavenly Father.

The truth is on many occasions we do good deeds either because people are watching or because of the obligation of some kind of responsibility. The truth is a lot of us have done a lot of good things with a very negative heart, which is why any positive energy we strive to emit has to start from the heart.

HOW SHOULD A CHRISTIAN RELY ON GOD?

Our Father in Heaven created all things, including we human beings. He created all our strengths and all our weaknesses. And it is written in the Bible that whatever we ask of him in his will, he will do for us.

Prayer is a powerful and essential tool needed to communicate with God. Through prayer we can glorify His name, thank Him for whatever He has done for us, and ask for His help and support.

However, when many Christians wield the power of prayer they forget that God has already provided many of the things that we ask for, day in and day out and hence fall into the trap of asking for the same thing over and over again, even after God has answered their requests.

Many Christians spend way too much time looking up instead of looking forward. For it is written in James 2 verse 17:

'Thus also faith by itself, if it does not have works, is dead.'

This means that a man who asks God to provide him with a job and then sits on his backside instead of actually looking for one is a joke in God's eyes. What I'm trying to say is: when one approaches God for help, he/she has to meet God halfway.

All through the Bible, God's word encourages us to pray, but with our prayers especially we have to be selfless. 10% of our prayers ideally should be about our personal needs and wants, while the other 90% of our prayers should be for people we can't physically help ourselves.

I also believe praying to God shouldn't always be formal and shouldn't always be about wanting something. I believe in literally approaching God with something like, 'What's up?' or 'How's it going up there in heaven?'

Think of God as a Father and an investor. Now imagine how an earthly Father would feel if every time you approached him you asked him for something. Of course it would bring a sense of hollowness to the relationship and an investor would only loan a set amount to start a business if he/she knew you were willing to bring everything else to get the business up and running.

A true sign that one has faith in God is when one isn't unnecessarily repetitive with one's prayer requests.

SHORT STORY 3

THE SCRIPTURE THAT GIVES MY CHRISTIANITY FOUNDATION

When I was asked by my Pastor how long I've been a Christian, he was surprised to hear me say ten years.

The truth is I have been a born-again Christian for more than ten years, however most of my life I have not been walking in the path of holiness.

The biggest reason for this is the fact that in the past I was under the conviction that as a born-again Christian, once you commit any sin, even if it took the form of an impure thought, you had to undergo a long and tedious spiritual ceremony before you could continue to call yourself a born-again Christian.

Then I came across Philippians 3 verse 13, which says:

'Brethren, I do not count myself to have apprehended; but one thing I do, forgetting those things which are behind and reaching forward to those things which are ahead.'

From this scripture, I learnt that as a born-again Christian as long as I was sincerely sorry and I asked God for forgiveness and help to overcome my sin, as well as make sure I took steps to ensure I didn't commit that sin again, I was still a born-again Christian and there was absolutely no need to dwell on my past sins or mistakes.

This is an important lesson for any born-again Christian because it is the first step to learning a vital lesson, which is spiritual growth is a never-ending journey.

POEM 3

REALITY CHECK.

A reality check is needed when two complete strangers meet for the first time and say they are in love.

A reality check is needed when one tries to find happiness without making other people happy.

A reality check is needed when people expect satisfaction in achievements they didn't really work for.

A reality check is needed when one believes in equal rights but has a problem with people openly expressing their opinions.

A reality check is needed for all those who believe that someday, under man's rule, the world will be a better place for everyone everywhere.

MANY CHRISTIANS ARE TOO RIGID

One of the most disturbing truths about many Christians is that they are too rigid. Rigid in the sense that they are unreasonably stubborn, inflexible, and they despise people who question the word of God, even if such questioning is in the context of innocently seeking a better understanding.

This rigid attitude, displayed by many Christians, is the very thing that once prevented me from giving my life to Christ. For such Christians portrayed this discipline as being uptight and judgemental.

The sad thing is that many Christians confuse rigidity with being spiritually aware, when in truth, there is a huge difference. Spiritual awareness is having an intimate relationship with God, while applying his word in your life. While being rigid is simply being religious, which is pointless since Christianity isn't a religion.

One of the major aims of a true Christian is to reach out to people. This is why being rigid is pointless as well as counter-productive because it is simply ridiculous to condemn every aspect of an individual one is trying to reach out to. Many Christians need to pick up the art of channelling the negative into the positive.

Jesus Christ himself utilised this way of thinking many times like in Matthew 8 verses 5 to 13 when a centurion asked him to heal his servant. Jesus Christ didn't at all focus on the centurion's sins, which were probably a truckload. Instead He focused on the fact that the centurion displayed a great deal of faith by coming to him. A rigid Christian would probably have put forward the notion that the centurion was unworthy to receive a miracle from Christ.

We as Christians have to be firm with the truth, which is the word of God, but at the same time we have to be flexible and wise.

HOW SELFLESS ARE CHRISTIANS?

To be selfless means putting other people's needs before your own or coming to the realisation that it isn't always about you. The ultimate example of selflessness is Jesus Christ dying for our sins.

However, many Christians are not selfless because a lot of the time they forget that the true objective of their lives is to positively reach out to people around them in more ways than one.

This lack of selflessness often rears its ugly head amongst Christians in the area of evangelism, for many Christians harbour a judgemental spirit and because of this believe, in terms of evangelizing, that certain individuals are off-limits, for example murderers, paedophiles, the mentally ill etc.

And when many Christians do decide to evangelize, they get so wrapped up in displaying their knowledge of the Bible that they lose sight of their main objective: which is to reach out rather than show off.

The above attitude causes many Christians to abandon the fact that the best form of evangelism is by meeting people at their needs and by establishing sincere friendships.

Jesus Christ displayed this technique many times by healing the sick and feeding the hungry. He also established a solid relationship with his disciples.

For a modern-day Christian, addressing someone's needs could be simply being there for someone in any way possible, be it physically, financially or spiritually. And reaching out to people through friendships could mean creating a fun weekly gathering that has a section dedicated to the gospel.

SHORT STORY 4

HAVING FAITH IN GOD AND HIS WORD

As Christians we would like to believe that we always have faith in God and his word, but in reality – for me anyway – this hasn't always been the case despite my attempt to be more spiritually aware.

When it comes to general things, like knowing God will in the end ensure everyone gets what they deserve, I haven't the slightest problem in having faith in God and his word.

Matthew 7 verse 24
'Therefore whoever hears these sayings of mine, and does them, I will liken him to a wise man who built his house on the rock;'

But in the past when it has come to believing in God for specific things, it has been extremely hard for me to maintain pure faith. A perfect example is when very recently I asked God to help mend a very valuable friendship. Now even though I knew such a task was nowhere near being beyond God, part of me couldn't help but doubt whether my prayers would be answered, because as far as my naked eye could see the friendship placed in front of me seemed beyond repair. However, despite my lack of total faith, God not only repaired the friendship, but also took it to a higher level.

The truth is, even though my faith in God hasn't always been impeccable, I've always believed – even when I wasn't a born-again Christian – that no matter how bad things may seem for me, God will always find a way to pull me through. But now that I'm a born- again Christian who has no intention of turning back, I know now that in terms of having faith in God and his word there is a lot of room for improvement.

POEM 4

EXTREMELY FAKE.

They laugh when they don't
Even understand the joke
They ask for a lighter
And they don't even smoke

They dance to music
Which they can't fathom the beat
They claim to be courageous
But when trouble comes they retreat

They pretend to be clever
But haven't got a clue
They try to be funny
But end up looking the fool

They are easily taken in
By what other people think
That's why in times of stress
Mentally they sink

No matter what shape or form
They may take
I can't stand people
Who are extremely fake

LOYALTY TO A LEADER

Many individuals (Christians included) believe becoming a leader means playing the role of boss and negatively skinny-dipping into a pool of authority.

The truth is a leader is simply a member of a team given the responsibility to ensure that a specific task or goal is carried out. The greatest leaders are willing to make the greatest sacrifices.

Jesus Christ put forward the notion in Mathew 20 verse 27 that to be a good leader one must be a good server.

'And whoever desires to be first among you, let him be your slave'

However, not everyone embraces this revelation. So knowing this, exactly how loyal do we stay to a leader?

The truth is ideally one should stay loyal to the task at hand and not the leader. For instance the task for a Christian is to embrace the word of God and spread it around. Now staying loyal to that task would mean supporting a Pastor to ensure a Church gathering reaches its full potential in terms of spreading the gospel.

Even if a leader is inadequate in his/her role, the follower should do everything in his/her power to support the head, before making a decision on whether or not to continue service under him/her.

Hebrews 13 verse 17
'Obey those who rule over you, and be submissive, for they watch out for your souls, as those who must give account.

Let them do so with joy and not with grief, for that would be unprofitable for you.'

For any task to be fruitful, one has to understand that having someone hold the role of a leader is extremely important in terms of managing or guiding through what needs to be done. However, a team as a whole is at its best when neither the leader nor the follower is solely interested in glory, power or recognition.

EFFECTS OF THE MEDIA ON CHILDREN RAISED IN WESTERN SOCIETY

An undeniable fact about today's western society is that sex, violence and various forms of obscene images are constantly thrown in our faces through movies, video games and music. And as much as many of us will hate to admit it, these images are unavoidable.

There is no denying that the media influences the behaviour of even fully-grown adults. Over the last thirty years, as images displayed on TV as well as the lyrics in songs have become more explicit, people in general have become more violent, sexually immoral and just plain crazy. The above is so rampant that very few things will faze the average thirteen year old that has been raised in a western country.

So after knowing all this, as Christians how do we raise our kids in today's western society? Well many Christians hold on to the Bible verses that say things like:

'Flee all appearances of evil.'

And then try to hide literally everything from their children, which is ridiculous seeing as their children will be exposed to these things the moment they step out of the house.

Christians first need to realise that spiritually they are soldiers for the Lord and then meditate on Bible verses like Luke 10 verse 19 that says:

'Behold, I give you the authority to trample on serpents and scorpions, and over all the power of the enemy, and nothing shall by any means hurt you.'

Now when a soldier is given the authority and ability to fight he/she can use his/her skills only when engaging the enemy. As far as the spiritual context is concerned in today's society Christians are surrounded and have absolutely no choice but to defend themselves.

The bottom line is, if an individual has a solid upbringing filled with love, practical guidance and the word of God, it will be virtually impossible for that young person to fall under the many bad influences around him/her.

Proverbs 22 verse 6
' Train up a child in the way he should go, and when he is old he will not depart from it.'

So parents, rather than being unnecessarily overprotective, love your children, respect them, and listen to their opinions no matter how silly or superficial they may be, but still be ready to discipline when necessary.

Parents should also explain every rule they put in place, for many army strategists believe that the best way for people to overcome their enemy is to know their enemy. So if for instance a mum should forbid her son from smoking, she should explain in detail the fact that it can affect his health negatively.

Parents should always ensure their children have a positive means of expressing themselves, because frustration of any kind is a powerful tool commonly manipulated by the devil.

Parents should also remember that God created absolutely everything and that anything evil is simply a creation of God tarnished by the devil. This means that anything negative could easily be transformed into something that is positive.

Being overprotective of your children is pointless and could prove to do more harm than good, for it creates a lot of room for clueless rebellion.

SHORT STORY 5

THE JOURNEY THAT IS SPIRITUAL GROWTH

Ever since I rededicated my life in 2003, I have made it a habit to ensure that every day that passes I make some kind of step towards spiritual growth.

One way I do this is by studying the Bible, which for me right now is consistent but random in terms of my study approach. I've also picked up the habit of constantly talking to God, especially now that I'm able to pray from the heart with a total disregard for language. For at one time I found it very hard to pray, but now anytime I'm faced with any kind of difficulty, I've picked up the habit of subtly praying on the spot.

In my quest for spiritual growth, I've also made it a habit to hang around individuals that are in some way or another very spiritually aware, which in many ways both directly and indirectly helps to put my spirit man in check.

I also try to mentally tune myself by thinking positively and nurturing a positive attitude that is aware that nothing can be done without God and that refuses to give up because of the simple fact that God will never give up on me.

I also endeavour to physically take care of myself by exercising regularly and staying away from things that can harm the body, such as smoking. However, I still need to develop myself in terms of my eating habits, because junk food still seems to be a good friend of mine.

I also fast a lot for various reasons, the major one being right now. I still feel like I have a truckload of bad habits to get rid of. And fasting for me is a way of constantly reminding myself that consciously turning back to any of my past bad habits or attitudes is not an option.

POEM 5

THE PAIN OF CARING

I give a helping hand
But it's quickly slapped away
I try and find the lost
But all they do is run away

I offer sincere friendship
But all they want is an enemy
I make a lot of sacrifices
And all they do is blame me

To these people I reach out daily
And in return my patience is put to the test
Most times all my efforts seem in vain
But all I can do is my best

CHRISTIANS SHOULDN'T HAVE KRYPTONITE

While growing up, one of my favorite comic book super heroes was Superman, for he was faster than a speeding bullet, stronger than a locomotive and – amongst other things – he could fly, plus he was virtually indestructible.

However he had one weakness that took the form of a green rock called Kryptonite. Any time Superman came in contact with this rock he became helpless, but as soon as he was not in any shape or form around it, he was super again.

Today many Christians have the Kryptonite mentality, meaning their way of overcoming their demons is simply by hiding from them, which is understandable considering in Matthew 5 verse 29–30
Jesus Christ taught us that:

'If your right eye causes you to sin, pluck it out and cast it from you; for it is more profitable for you that one of your members perish, than for your whole body to be cast in hell.'

The above scripture shouldn't be taken lightly especially if you've just begun to do battle with demons that take the form of bad habits. However Christians also have to remember Bible verses like Luke 10 verse 19 that says:

'Behold, I give you the authority to trample on serpents and scorpions, and over all the power of the enemy, and nothing shall by any means hurt you.'

Also remember the constant emphasis on faith throughout God's word. If so far I've made absolutely no sense then let me put it like this: if an alcoholic man can only stay sober when liquor is hidden from him, then he is still an alcoholic even if liquor stays hidden from him for over a hundred years.

As Christians we haven't truly defeated our demons until we are able to laugh in their faces and say, *'nice try'*.

So as a Christian, if night-clubbing caused you to sin in the past then you should aim to reach a stage with your spiritual growth whereby you can enter a nightclub and overcome all temptation with ease.

But some may ask questions like 'why bother reaching this level?' and 'Isn't attempting to reach this level just giving sin more opportunity to have dominion over us?'

First of all, no Christian should attempt facing their demons head on like this until they are filled with God's word and the Holy Spirit, which will only come from building a true intimate relationship with God through prayer and studying the Bible.

Second of all, it is necessary for all Christians to reach this level because if we as Christians possess a kryptonite, we will limit ourselves substantially in terms of reaching out to people and growing spiritually as individuals.

To put things in perspective, just imagine how useless Superman would be in a world made out of Kryptonite.

WHY I DISLIKE THE TERM 'SECULAR WORLD'

Many Christians use the term 'secular' to describe anything that hasn't been produced and propagated by an individual or group of individuals to directly glorify the name of Jesus Christ, be it the creation of movies, music or literature.

Using the above term is understandable because once an individual gives his/her life to Christ he/she becomes very different when compared to the unbelieving world around him/her. Also the term 'secular' has its merits because it helps keeps Christians in check by reminding them that living a certain kind of lifestyle can compromise their spiritual growth. It is written in 1 John 2 verse 15 that:

'Do not love the world or the things in the world. If anyone loves the world, the love of the father is not in him.'

The above scripture to some extent explains the need for many Christians to constantly separate the believers from the non-believers even when it comes to the nature of their creativity.

However, man's habit of unnecessarily segregating things in a negative context is the major reason why morally he is digressing at a rapid rate and is why mankind as a whole hasn't positively reached its full potential economically and technologically.

Christians have to remember that as much as there is a lot of evil in the world, there is a lot of good in the world that simply needs to be topped up with the fact that Jesus Christ is our Lord and personal saviour, through whom alone can we enter the kingdom of Heaven. I dislike the term 'secular' because I believe to some extent Christians use the term to kill this fact. Also it is written that:

'He that is in you is greater than he that is in the world.'

This is another reminder to me that anything bad in the world is simply a creation of God tarnished by the devil, which is why as a Christian I would not condemn something simply because it doesn't directly glorify God.

SHORT STORY 6

TALKING TO GOD

Prayer has always been an important part of my life even when the term 'born-again Christian' was a 'dirty word' to me. Praying consistently was a habit I picked up from a very early age and it was one I kept right into adulthood.

However there were many periods in my life when I went without prayer for very long periods of time, because I was in some way or another consumed by my own sin and felt too guilty to go back to God, or because my prayers in themselves didn't feel real or potent, which I guess was rooted in my subconscious lack of faith.

Now as a born-again Christian, prayer has become second nature to me, especially now that I can speak in tongues, which is simply praying from the heart with a total disregard for language.

Now I pray at any time, all the time and because I pray from the heart, I'm 100% certain that every time I pray there is effective communication with God.

Sin, in many ways, is still a hindrance to my prayer because when I sin it is hard for me not to doubt my worthiness or ability to talk to God. But thanks to *Philippians 3 verse 13,* a scripture I keep close to my heart, that doubt now lasts a maximum of 3 seconds. I however make it a point not to consciously take advantage of God's mercy.

POEM 6

ADULTHOOD

People I grew up with are married
And are now fully pledged parents
People I grew up with are in jail
Creating huge emotional dents

My age mates are in university
Getting their degrees
My age mates are famous
Getting a handsome fee

My age mates are rising to the challenge
And facing their fears
My age mates have set out
To start real careers

My heroes have subconsciously revealed
Their many flaws
From my heroes I now expect
Far much more

No matter how I deny it
It does me no good
So I've grown to except
I've entered the world of Adulthood

LIES

A lie can be defined as deliberately putting forward an untrue notion with the intent to deceive.

Many Christians believe the most rampant sin in today's society is fornication, but the truth is the most common sin to date is the lie.
The sad truth is that we lie all the time in many ways.

There is of course the direct or conscious lie that is easy to pick out and condemn and is usually displayed by con artists.

There is the indirect lie, which can simply take the form of an individual supporting a lie already told or orchestrating one without actually telling it directly. This is very common when carrying out pranks or dodgy schemes.

People also lie out of ignorance. This is usually a by-product of someone else's lie.

Then there is the kind lie, which is often used to spare people's feelings or make others feel better about themselves.

We even have the subconscious lie, which is usually when people lie to themselves to avoid a harsh reality.

The lie is so embedded in our society that many people believe the act is now an unavoidable necessity, which is sadly a lie in itself for it is simply another impure act that the devil has managed to desensitize us to.

The lie is Satan's most powerful weapon and if nurtured can destroy a man in many ways. For starters it can hide the real you. Many people are kept away from greatness or prosperity because in some way lies have hidden away a unique gift they can bring to the world. The lie has the power to imprison a man in a problem for a whole lifetime. A lie can discourage a man from pursuing a dream or saving a life.

So how do we avoid the lie, because I for one have found myself telling lies almost by reflex.

Well, first of all, we have to accept the fact that initially avoiding the lie would probably be the most difficult task of our lives. But like everything else we take on board, after a while it will become second nature to us especially if we go to God for help through prayer.

Then we have to eliminate every ounce of unnecessary pride we have because pride often breeds all sorts of lies. We would also have to eliminate every ounce of laziness because this is a spirit that often pushes us to lie even to ourselves.

Then we start by being brutally honest with ourselves about everything by simply viewing everything as it is (call a spade a spade) and by adopting the habit of being open about everything including the fact that we do not wish to share certain things with certain people.

Apart from the lie having a negative impact on the spiritual being, one will find if one adopts the habit of being 100% honest one will attain a high form of peace. Also, it will be easier for one to gain self-respect within oneself as well as amongst people around even in the midst of those that hate one.

THE ART OF GIVING

There have been many debates about how one should contribute towards one's Church gatherings and ones's Charities.

Some say not giving to those less fortunate than yourself is a sin, others say not paying your tithes and offering to your Church gathering is the equivalent of robbing God. While others say it isn't compulsory to give to the Church or the needy.

Well, the bottom line is: giving is good for the body, mind and soul, and the more you give the more you receive.

Now, if you view the above words as being corny with no real substance then I challenge you outright to do a survey.

For the first half of this survey, I challenge you to check any man or woman (whether they are famous or not) that is sincerely loved by people around him/her. You will find that this person has either made some kind of sacrifice either with his/her money, time, sweat or blood or he/she has a natural flair for showing kindness to people around him/her.

For the second half of this survey, I challenge you to check any man or woman who feels lonely, unloved, or unwanted. I guarantee you will find that this individual has either never loved or shown kindness to anyone or at one point stopped showing love and kindness to people around him/her.

In 1 Kings chapter 3 verses 4–15, King Solomon made a huge offering to God, which in turn provoked the Lord, causing the son of David to get a visitation. When God gave Solomon the chance to make a blessing request, Solomon asked for the chance to rule his people with wisdom and this again provoked God to release even more blessings upon Solomon's life.

There are two lessons to be learnt from this story. The first lesson is that every time you give, in some way or another God will reward you. The second lesson is that the best kind of giving is the selfless kind. Selfless giving is when one gives with no real intent of being rewarded or repaid.

Solomon, even during his moment of being rewarded, was still displaying a giving heart, for his request was for a tool to help bring prosperity to his people.

People in general need to come to the revelation that there is a season to give and a season to receive.

POEM 7

GENUINELY NICE.

To a stranger they will greet
Like that person genuinely exists
King, beggar or criminal
To show respect they can't resist

To make a positive difference
These people will try more than thrice
Why? Because these people give from the heart
And are genuinely nice

FINDING MR/MRS RIGHT

Proverbs 18 verse 22
'He who finds a wife finds a good thing, and obtains favour from the Lord.'

The above scripture proves that God himself approves of us as human beings, finding a partner to share our entire lives, within the context of marriage.

The idea of marriage in its right and purest form is beautiful, for it means giving and receiving love with a member of the opposite sex that accepts you for you and in some way or the other pushes you to better yourself as a person.

However, the act of marriage, like many other beautiful acts, has been abused without mercy by today's society. For in today's society many people marry for the wrong reasons mainly because of three things, which are:

1. Greed
2. Fear
3. Indiscipline

1. Marrying out of greed is actually one of the most common reasons for the abuse of marriage, for many people nowadays marry just to obtain money, fame or status, which is extremely sad.

2. Fear too is a common reason for abusing marriage especially amongst females. For fear of being alone often causes men and women to rush into marriage without even checking to see whether they have chosen the right partner.

3. Another common reason for abusing the act of marriage is indiscipline within an individual, which often leads to people marrying solely because of passion, chemistry or physical attraction.

The truth is that many people actually find the right partner but still make the wrong decision, and this is because they don't take their time to enjoy every stage (friendship – courtship – engagement – marriage). Many people – Christians included – like the idea of skipping a stage or two.

In terms of the road to marriage, everyone's timeline is different, but for anyone to get married to anyone they've known for less than a year is too hasty and not advisable.

A relationship that leads to marriage should go beyond anything physical or material and should be built on sincere friendship and sincere love, because if it isn't, it will either die prematurely or it will orchestrate a lifetime of unhappiness.

SEX

Jesus Christ preached in Matthew 5 verse 28 that *'whoever looks at a woman to lust for her has already committed adultery with her in his heart.'*

Yet sexual immortality in this day and age seems to be the norm. Millions of people have sex before marriage, the market for pornography seems to be growing rapidly, and homosexuality has been deemed by a substantial proportion of the world as being acceptable.

It is hard to be surprised by the above facts, especially if you've been alive for the last twenty years. Sexual immorality has been glossed up by the media in so many ways, which in turn has caused many people to even aspire to be sexually immoral.

Sex nowadays is used to sell everything from cars to video games to even a cup of coffee. In fact, in this day and age, it is harder than ever to conduct yourself according to the will of God in a sexual context, especially if you're a man. In fact, in western society, I think it's practically impossible to go through the day without seeing a half naked woman.

However, the fact that it is so easy to be sexually immoral should be in itself an incentive to keep oneself sexually pure because doing the right thing sexually would challenge the ideals of many individuals and change them for the better.

God created sex to help celebrate marriage and create the gift of childbirth. Every time sex is practiced outside marriage then the creation of God is tainted.

SHORT STORY 7

WINNING SOULS FOR CHRIST

There was a time in my life when I wanted nothing to do with evangelism because my view of winning souls for Christ was standing in the middle of the street screaming out –

'The Kingdom of God is at hand.'

It was only when I began to realise that one could be as creative as possible as far as evangelism was concerned, that I began to adopt my own style to win souls for Christ.

The technique I have adopted usually involves my steering people away from bad habits with advice, support – or both – through establishing a genuine friendship of some kind. This could mean my being a mentor, mediator or agony aunt.

I have found through observation and experience that effective evangelism can only come by understanding an individual's needs, which will involve a lot of listening as well as a lot of talking.

POEM 8

THE BOTTOM LINE.

There are people I know
That are genuinely good
And dedicate their lives
To helping others

There are people I know
That are consumed with greed
Those that consider nothing and no one
Except for the things they claim to need

Whatever kind of person you are
Whatever life you serve
Remember in the end
We all get what we deserve

LEAP OF FAITH

The official definition of faith amongst even those that choose to stay outside the teachings of Jesus Christ is 'trust in God'.

Faith is an extremely powerful tool that, believe it or not, is used every day in many ways. Faith in the form of self-belief is something that has caused ordinary men to do great things. However, the most powerful form of faith in existence is faith in God.

A man that has faith in God can move mountains and vanquish entire armies. But having faith in God isn't just an admission, it's something that will show in your words and actions. Someone who truly has faith in God will display it by living a life that glorifies God because they know that God's word can never lie and that as long as they live in God's word they will prosper.

Jesus Christ is a prime example of this, for his ability to allow God to perform miracles through him was because he lived a life that honoured God and he had faith along with a relationship with God's word. This was why Satan's attempt to tempt him was absolutely futile.

Matthew 4 verse 4
... 'It is written "Man shall not live by bread alone, but by every word that proceeds from the mouth of God." '

If a man doesn't have faith in God, he ties the hands of God in the context of his life. Just like in Matthew 13 verse 58 when Jesus Christ was unable to do many mighty works in his hometown because of the people's unbelief. This scripture is just one of many in the Bible that illustrates the power of faith and the detrimental effect of the lack of faith.

The very nature of free will that exists within man gives him the ability to embrace God or to keep the Lord outside his life. And the choice between the two is simply determined by faith.

MASTURBATION

Masturbation, an act that could be defined as self-induced sexual pleasure via stroking of the genitals, is something many people laugh at yet it is something many people practice.

Many so-called sex experts claim that masturbating is harmless and is in fact good for the body for it relieves sexual frustration that could lead to unwanted pregnancy or sexually transmitted diseases.

However several English dictionaries have defined the act as self-abuse, which in a way explains why many disciplines believe the act reduces the body's energy considerably.

Whether we like it or not, adultery is a sin, and Jesus Christ pointed out in Matthew 5 verse 28 that once a man even looks at a woman lustfully an act of adultery has already been committed. Masturbation is simply an act of adultery taken further.

Masturbation is actually a serious disease with serious consequences physically, mentally and spiritually. An individual who chooses to let the spirit of masturbation rule him/her is in danger of facing the same kind of loneliness and inner turmoil as an alcoholic or drug addict. Yet the act is encouraged by the media in more ways than one, especially through the pornographic industry.

The truth is that the first step to defeat masturbation on a wider scale is by making it publicly known that it is a damaging act.

SHORT STORY 8

MY MEMBERSHIP OF MY CHURCH

Other people would class me as a member of my Church gathering for different reasons. My Pastor would probably say something like I'm a member because God sent me to the Church gathering, while the average observer would say because I have physically, spiritually and financially contributed immensely to help build various aspects of the Church gathering.

I however see myself as a member simply because I care. And because I care it is automatically shown through my actions. However if I fell ill or moved far away, I would still see myself as a member because I would always remember the gathering in my prayers.

Why do I care? Partly because of my choice to be a born-again Christian, but mainly because I see the Church gathering as a great tool to reach out to people in the surrounding communities in more ways than one.

POEM 9

FRAGILE.

Strong, independent and as friendly
As they come
Amongst my friends
I'm the most dominant one

Physically I'm fit
And as solid as a rock
On all my goals I have a focus
And a serious mental lock

Physically and mentally stable
From a distance I may seem
But I tell you it takes very little
To hurt and upset me

MIXED MOTIVES BEHIND PREACHING

Since even before Jesus Christ died for our sins, many men have gone out of their way to preach the goodness of our Father in Heaven.

This became even more intense after Jesus Christ came and taught the word of God, then empowered his disciples with the Holy Spirit before finally sending them out to spread the gospel.

God has used many men to preach the gospel and in turn billions over countless generations have been healed and saved, spiritually and physically.

However, man's natural wicked habit to abuse any positive act doesn't exclude the preaching of the word of God. For many individuals go into ministry for their own personal gain. This was touched on in 1 Timothy 1 verses 5–8:

'Now the purpose of the commandment is love from a pure heart, from a good conscience, and from sincere faith, from which some, having strayed, have turned aside to idle talk, desiring to be teachers of the law, understanding neither what they say nor the things which they affirm.'

Jesus Christ on several occasions touched on the fact that many hypocrites would appear to be sincere men of God.

Matthew 15 verses 8–9
'These people draw near to me with their mouth, and honor me with their lips, but their heart is far from me.'

Such individuals have served as convenient excuses for many people to backslide into their old negative habits or not to give their lives to Christ at all.

Many hypocrites or wrongly spirited preachers tend to teach doctrines that do not please God, while some actually stick with the undiluted word of God. This is why, as Christians, we have to be aware of the fact that although it is important to commune with other true Christians in a Church environment, the true essence of our faith should be derived from an intimate relationship built upon prayer and the study of the word, for this in itself will help us differentiate between fact and fiction.

THE ART OF RELIGION

Religion could easily be defined as man's search for God, and over the ages man has followed all sorts of religions.

Now it is easy to point out religions that logically just can't take you to heaven, and they usually come under the category of religions that promote violence. But from a logical standpoint it is hard to fault religions that preach peace and goodwill to all men.

The truth is no religion can take you to heaven simply because religion is what man can do for God. Now it is written in the Bible that a man's righteousness is like filthy rags in the sight of the Lord. This means there is no amount of good deeds a man can display with his own strength that will impress God.

Apart from that, if God was to grade those that entered heaven based simply on deeds then no one will ever see the kingdom of God because it is impossible for man not to sin simply because he is drenched in it. One could sin simply with a thought that lasted for a split second.

This is why Christianity isn't a religion, for it is God's search for man. Christianity is basically a state of mind that allows one to have an intimate relationship with God.

Some may argue that praying and studying the Bible are in themselves religious acts. However just because salvation is given to one free of charge doesn't mean it shouldn't be maintained. Plus building a relationship with God, although it should be consistent, doesn't have to be rigid; hence the reasons for many methods of praying and studying the Bible.

Religious acts without an intimate relationship with God are basically a waste of time even amongst Christians. The only way one can have an intimate relationship with God is through following the teachings of Jesus Christ with a sincere and humble heart.

SHORT STORY 9

FINAL NOTE TO A COLLEAGUE

Officially, I'm just moving on to work on another project for a while, but in truth this may be the last time you and I work together.

Now the truth is that according to the mentality of most people I have a truckload of reasons to despise you as a person, but the truth is that I shouldn't be thinking like most people.

This is why I'm ashamed to say that on a conscious level I have tried to stop God from using me to answer a lot of your questions.

The truth is that, despite my attempts, God still managed to take over my subconscious and use me to touch your heart while I was trying to reach out to the young people under us and while I had the odd deep conversation with you.

Christianity has taught me that in our day-to-day lives we aren't really facing the evil of man, but the evil of spirits and principalities that use man, which is why I had no right to spiritually turn my back on you simply because of your behaviour.

So as we seem to go our separate ways, I just want you to know that if you need to talk about anything that is bringing you down on any level be it physically, emotionally or financially feel free to contact me.

Take care of yourself.

POEM 10

EVIL.

It's around our children
On the streets
It's in our churches
Amongst our priests

While they teach our kids
It's amongst school teachers
While they're debating politics
It's amongst the world leaders

You might not see
But it's behind the odd smile
Just wait, it's coming
Give it a while

Many may not believe it
But it's the reason why life isn't fair
To shield against it you must accept
That evil is everywhere

DREAMS IN YOUR SLEEP

When many people hear the phrase 'God spoke to me' the first image that pops into their head is of clouds opening and a loud voice that vibrates the whole earth while speaking.

The truth is that God speaks to us through many mediums such as the Holy Spirit – who is a lot more convicting than your conscience – through friends, people in general and through his word (the Holy Bible).

Another medium through which God speaks to us is through our dreams. Through our dreams, God tells us how he feels about us or what he has planned for our lives. Examples of this are displayed throughout the Bible as in the lives of Solomon, Jacob and Joseph.

Many people are quick to disregard dreams saying they are simply residual images left behind in our subconscious, which to some extent is very true. If a man watched a superhero movie and then dreamt about being a superhero that very night then I would have to agree with the residual image theory. However, if the images dreamt about haven't really been dwelt upon by the person in question, then I would have to say they definitely represent some kind of meaningand are messages from God.

Take the 'pharaoh dream' interpreted by God through Joseph in the Bible. The ruler of Egypt dreamt about a thin cow, which when interpreted represented famine.

Dreams are also tools used by the devil and his minions to tempt us or tarnish our souls in some way. Many stories

64

have depicted individuals being initiated into dark evil cults through dreams.

At this point, a few people may wonder how it is that one can differentiate a dream sent by God from a dream sent by the devil.

The answer to that is 'I don't know', but build a relationship with God and you'll find out.

SHOULD WE ALWAYS BLAME THE DEVIL?

When Adam gave in to sin by disobeying God and eating the forbidden fruit, he sold the world to the devil.

This is why Satan currently rules the world, which in itself explains all the horrific things that happen today.

However, God has given us free will and Jesus Christ has died for our sins. These facts reduce the devil to nothing more than a salesman.

When we walk into a shop, the salesperson can only market and advertise their products the best they can, but can't actually force us to buy anything.

The phrase '*I didn't really have a choice*' is used a lot, but the truth is we always have a choice. The simple truth is in many circumstances the right choice is the hard choice.

It is written, '*He that is in you is greater than he that is in the world*'. This statement basically depicts the fact that if you put your trust in God with your heart and actions the world as we know it will never be able to break you.

The devil can only be blamed for setting up the shop, but in terms of walking in to make a purchase, we're always to blame no matter how big or small the purchase.

SHORT STORY 10

DEAR YOUNG PERSON

I'm writing you this letter not because officially I have to but because, before you head out into the real world, I would really like you to listen to one more session of the Joseph Johnson preaching.

I know I may have come across harsh, sometimes so much so there are times you probably thought I was fed up or I didn't even like you, but the truth is I saw so much potential in you, and it frustrated me that you were not using your talents to the full.

So before we kind of part ways, I want you to take the following as rules to live your life by:

1. Have fun, work hard, but always put first what is important
    (Like family and real friends).
2. Think before you act.
3. Treat others the way you want to be treated.
4. Never be afraid to ask questions.
5. Create a plan to pursue your dreams.
6. Never give up.
7. Never feel sorry for yourself.
8. Never think the world owes you anything.
9. Live your life for yourself and not for others.
10. Learn to buckle down sometimes even if the task isn't fun.
11. Smile or laugh at least twenty times a day.

If you need anything, even if it is someone to talk to, feel free to contact me, for I may be blunt or even harsh at times but I will never judge you. I will never look down on you and I will never give up on you because, believe it or not, no matter where you go or what you do, I will always see a person capable of achieving great things.

POEM 11

MAN AS A DISEASE.

We destroy vast forests
To build our cities
We destroy beautiful habitats for our wants
Showing no pity

Animals needlessly die
To decorate our sitting rooms
For our pleasure
Nature needlessly faces its doom

We contaminate our water
Through dumping because we can't be bothered
We contaminate our air
Then blame it on each other

It wouldn't surprise me
If nature made us pay our debt
For man truly is
The cancer of this planet

USING SATAN'S WEAPONS AGAINST HIM

'Be as wise as a serpent and as harmless as a dove'.
The above is a lesson taught by Jesus Christ, which many Christians neglect or even condemn.

The most effective combat principle ever to exist is one that encourages you to use your attacker's strength or advantage against him/her. This principle, if mastered, would mean an individual would be able to defeat any opponent regardless of his/her strengths. This principle is something many Christians have refused to adopt because they are too busy condemning everything.

Many Christians say rock music is evil, but once such a theory is accepted then how would you reach the millions of people in love with rock music. The truth is any genre of music can be used to praise God, because the essence of any song lies in its lyrics.

As I've mentioned before, instead of over-thinking things while embracing the spirits of fear and self-righteousness, Christians need to learn how to take absolutely any negative and turn it into a positive.

A few examples could be: instead of labelling a Martial arts expert as an advocate of violence, encourage the expert to use his/her strong sense of discipline to contribute to the work of God: instead of a Christian filmmaker refusing to make a violent movie, he/she should make a violent movie with subliminal messages which encourage the ways of Christ, because whether we like it or not there are people that will only watch violent movies.

Every time an art form or hobby is unnecessarily condemned, then millions of people are hindered or delayed from taking in the very essence of Jesus Christ's teaching, which is love.

SPIRITUAL BLACKMAIL

2 Timothy 4 verse 3
'For the time will come when they will not endure sound doctrine, but according to their own desires, because they have itching ears, they will heap up for themselves teachers'

Many Christians will read the above scripture and automatically assume it applies to all those that don't believe in Jesus Christ.
The truth is that it applies to every single individual in more ways than one.

Many people including Christians are guilty of spiritual blackmail, which is basically the false manipulation of God's word to persuade people to fulfil an individual or selfish need.

Yes, it is true God speaks to us all the time, but many Christians including Pastors love to use the phrase 'God told me' or 'God showed me' when in truth, at the time, God didn't tell them or show them anything.

Spiritual blackmail is the reason why we have many false faiths that are centred solely on religious acts. Spiritual blackmail is what fuels every single extremist that acts in the name of a god.

Spiritual blackmail is something we should all stay far away from because immediately one gets caught in such a habit, that person is not only using God's name to be deceitful but on a subconscious level that individual is claiming to be smarter than the Lord Almighty, which is dangerous, for it's written in 1 Corinthians 1 verse 25:

'The foolishness of God is wiser than men'

Spiritual blackmail is Satan's stealth jet for through it he grabs holds of many people's hearts with ease. Again, I will point out having a sincere personal relationship with God will help protect you from anything that will pull you astray.

SHORT STORY 11

A NOTE TO A PASTOR

First of all I would like to take this opportunity to thank you for presenting me the opportunity to exercise various skills within your church by allowing me to hold several responsibilities.

In recent months, as much as I have tried to ignore the feeling, deep down the events that have led to our brother's departure from the house of God have deeply troubled me. I have an extremely hard time accepting the church's decision to allow him to leave for three main reasons:

1. I strongly believe whatever an individual's problem, whether it involves him having a negative attitude or being possessed by evil spirits, the house of God should go out of its way to fix the individual and not discard him/her. Especially if this individual is going out of his/her way to create peace and strive towards the church's ultimate goal, which is to save souls.

2. God has given your church a mandate to reach hundreds of people. Our brother is a young man who despite his personal shortcomings has an incredible God-given gift, which has the potential of changing many people's lives for the better. Allowing our brother to walk away is like asking God for food and then slapping his hand away when he gives us bread.

3. I strongly believe winning souls is not an art or a science and hence should not involve Christians

74

taking on the role of hardcore economists or politicians while carrying out the responsibility. Instead, when trying to win souls, as Christians we should aim to be selfless right down to the very fibre of our being and eliminate the whole notion of any evil entity sneaking through the backdoor. For if we as Christians do what is right in the eyes of the Lord, then absolutely no evil can prosper against us.

On a plain personal note I wouldn't have even bothered commenting on the matter, but as a man striving for spiritual growth I believe it would have been wrong, if I didn't make it very clear that I was in total disagreement with the outcome of the entire episode.

This note isn't designed to change your view on the matter, and is instead just a means of letting you know how I feel about the issue.

Yours Truly
Church member

PS: I was the one that pushed our brother to write you a letter this week and to book an appointment to see you.

POEM 12

TRUE FRIENDSHIP.

When we don't hesitate
To give each other advice
Run to each other's aid
Whether it's day or night

When we have a lot in common
And generally have a laugh
In each other's company we are not scared
To act stupid or incredibly daft

And in time of great difficulty
If we don't let each other slip
Then we can say
We have experienced true friendship

THE BOTTOM LINE

The collection of simple thoughts you have just read is not intended to judge or look down upon anyone, because in truth I, the writer, am guilty of doing many of the negative acts highlighted in the previous pages. This book however is intended to point out a few things that, like it or not, do not please God or benefit us in the long run.

The truth is that the only way to prosper and find peace in any world is to accept Jesus Christ as your Lord and personal saviour, and to build a relationship with God. A good way to find out why and how to do this is to start by asking yourself three questions:

1. Why should I love God?
2. How do I know he loves me?
3. How do I know he's fair?

The answers to all the above are pretty straight forward:

1. God sent his only begotten son to die on the cross for all our sins. And all the teachings given by his son if followed would guarantee emotional, mental, physical, financial, and spiritual prosperity. In Proverbs 11 verse 5, it points out the fact that the wicked will fall by their own wickedness. This, if looked at carefully, points out the fact that with every sin is attached some kind of negative consequence that harms the body, mind and soul. Don't believe me? Then I challenge you to honestly attach a consequence to any sin you can think of.

2. The Bible clearly illustrates the fact that God loves you dearly, which is why he is constantly ready to forgive you for your sins.

3. God has given us free will, which means although he advises us what to do and tells us the consequences of our actions, he doesn't force us to do anything.

As mentioned before, a relationship with God, like any other relationship, should involve sincerity. This means constantly sharing how you feel with God whether you feel guilty, sad, inadequate, angry, or lost. Then go through the Bible to see what God says regarding these feelings, for God has touched on every issue you can think of with his word.

If you've read this book and you feel the urge to give your life to Christ for the first time or you feel the need to rededicate your life to Christ then all you have to do is give a simple prayer that basically says:

'God, I'm truly sorry for all the sins I've committed against you. Please forgive me and have mercy on my soul.I now accept Jesus Christ as my Lord and personal saviour and will begin to do all that I can to live a life that will please you.'

Amen.

Once you recite this prayer you have instantly received a free gift of salvation, which like any other gift to be used daily has to be maintained by:

1. Finding a comfortable way to talk to God through prayer.

2. Finding a comfortable way to study his word/the Bible.
3. Finding a way to comfortably interact with other born-again Christians.

SPIRITUAL WARFARE

Spiritual warfare for me goes beyond praying, fasting or quoting scriptures. The essence of Spiritual warfare in my opinion lies in standing your ground in Christ, which is choosing to hold onto the true Christian faith no matter what the circumstance.

The ideal setting for the above formula is Christians staying clear away from iniquity. However, the truth is that spiritual warfare takes place in various forms or on various battlefields.

Another example of spiritual warfare other than the one given above is Christians going head to head with demons, evil spirits or curses through prayer, praise and worship and fasting. This is usually the first example that jumps into people's heads when they hear the term spiritual warfare.

Being able to spiritually-apologise to God is another example of spiritual warfare. A spiritual apology is basically saying sorry to God and actually meaning it from the heart. Many Christians backslide because they follow the myth that some sins are unforgivable in the sight of God, when in truth the Lord is willing to forgive anyone with a sincere heart. Being able to admit you're wrong and apologise to God is definitely a victory on both a physical and spiritual level.

Having faith in God is also like going to war on a spiritual level. In fact, having and maintaining faith is the foundation of any battle you will face as a Christian, be it having faith enough to walk in the path of holiness, believing God will deliver on an issue, or knowing God has given us as Christians the power to overcome any principality or power.

My personal spiritual weapon lies in <u>Philippians 3 verse 13</u> which says:

'Brethren, I do not count myself to have apprehended; but one thing I do, forgetting those things which are behind and reaching forward to those things which are ahead'

This scripture has on countless occasions prevented evil desires and entities from getting the best of me, because it constantly reminds me that my path to spiritual growth can't be destroyed unless I totally give up on my relationship with God.

Ecclesiastes 7 verse 16—18

Do not be overly righteous
Nor be overly wise:
Why should you destroy yourself?
Do not be overly wicked,
Nor be foolish:
Why should you die before your time?
It is good that you grasp this,
And also remove your hand from the other;
For he who fears God will escape them all.

SOME SCRIPTURES TO MEDITATE UPON

- Ecclesiastes 7 verse 16–18

- 1 John 5 verse 13

- Joshua 1 verse 8

- Matthew 10 verse 16

- Matthew 13 verse 57

- Matthew 15 verse 8–9

- Matthew 19 verse 21

- Matthew 23 verse 1–3

- Thessalonians 5 verse 12–the end of the chapter

- Genesis 32 verse 22–the end of the chapter

- Acts 9

- Acts 14 verse 11–15

- Romans 1 verse 17

- Romans 2 verse 1

- Romans 2 verse 12–16

- Romans 2 verse 25–29

- Romans 3 verse 23

- Romans 8 verse 31–32

- Romans 12 verse 2

- Romans 14 verse 13

- Romans 16 verse 19

- 1 Corinthians 1 verse 21

- 1 Corinthians 1 verse 25

- 1 Corinthians 1 verse 27

- 1 Corinthians 2 verse 5

- 1 Corinthians 3 verse 18

- 1 Corinthians 4 verse 5

- 1 Corinthians 9 verse 10

- 1 Corinthians 12 verse 7–11

- 1 Corinthians 13 verse 1

- 1 Corinthians 15 verse 33–34

- 2 Corinthians 1 verse 1–4

- 2 Corinthians 9 verse 6

- Galatians 3 verse 26–29

- Galatians 4 verse 9–11

- Galatians 5 verse 4

- Galatians 5 verse 16

- Galatians 6 verse 3

- Galatians 6 verse 4–5

- Galatians 6 verse 9

- Galatians 6 verse 10

- Ephesians 4 verse 26–29

- Ephesians 5 verse 3–5

- Ephesians 5 verse 18

- Ephesians 5 verse 22–33

- Ephesians 6 verse 1–3

- Ephesians 6 verse 4

- Ephesians 6 verse 5

- Ephesians 6 verse 12

- Philippians 2 verse 14

- Philippians 3 verse 1

- Philippians 3 verse 13

- Philippians 3 verse 16

- Philippians 4 verse 6–7

- Philippians 4 verse 11

- Philippians 4 verse 13

- Philippians 4 verse 19

- Colossians 2 verse 3

- Colossians 2 verse 8

- Colossians 3 verse 5

- Colossians 3 verse 8

- Colossians 3 verse 11

- Colossians 3 verse 12–15

- Colossians 3 verse 18

- Colossians 3 verse 19

- Colossians 3 verse 20

- Colossians 3 verse 21

- Colossians 4 verse 1

- 1 Thessalonians 4 verse 4–5

- 1 Thessalonians 5 verse 18

- 1 Thessalonians 5 verse 19

- 2 Thessalonians 2 verse 9–13

- 2 Thessalonians 3 verse 6–10

- 1 Timothy 1 verse 6–8

- 1 Timothy 2 verse 3–5

- 1 Timothy 3 verse 1–14

- 1 Timothy 3 verse 16

- 1 Timothy 6 verse 10

- 2 Timothy 1 verse 7

- 2 Timothy verse 1–5

- 2 Timothy 4 verse 4

- 2 Timothy 4 verse 18

- Titus 1 verse 16

- Titus 2 verse 6–9

- Hebrews 2 verse 18

- Hebrews 3 verse 13

- Hebrews 5 verse 12

- Hebrews 6 verse 10

- Hebrews 10 verse 26–28

- Hebrews 13 verse 1–2

- Hebrews 13 verse 8

- Hebrews 13 verse 15–16

- James 1 verse 5

- James 1 verse 6–8

- James 1 verse 9–11

- James 1 verse 12–18

- James 1 verse 19–20

- James 1 verse 22

- James 1 verse 26–27

- James 2 verse 1–4

- James 2 verse 10

- James 2 verse 13

- James 2 verse 17

- Proverbs 1 verse 5

- Proverbs 1 verse 7

- Proverbs 1 verse 24–27

- James 4 verse 7

- Proverbs 3 verse 1–2

- Proverbs 3 verse 5

- Proverbs 3 verse 9

- Proverbs 3 verse 11–12

- Proverbs 3 verse 25

- Proverbs 3 verse 27

- Proverbs 3 verse 30

- James 5 verse 7

- James 5 verse 12

- James 5 verse 20

- Psalm 4 verse 4

- Psalm 4 verse 8

- Proverbs 5 verse 3–6

- 1 John 1 verse 6

- 1 Johns 1 verse 8

- Proverbs 6 verse 16–19

- 1 Peter 1 verse 13–17

- 1 Peter 1 verse 18–19

- 1 Peter 3 verse 1–4

- 1 Peter 3 verse 7

- 1 Peter 3 verse 8

- Proverbs 8 verse 36

- 1 Peter 4 verse 4–6

- 1 Peter 4 verse 8

- 1 Peter 4 verse 15

- Proverbs 9 verse 7

- Proverbs 9 verse 8

- Proverbs 9 verse 10

- Psalm 8 verse 4

- Psalm 8 verse 5

- 1 Peter 5 verse 1–5

- 1 Peter 5 verse 6–7

- Proverbs 10 verse 14

- Proverbs 10 verse 18

- Proverbs 10 verse 23

- Psalm 10 verse 23

- Psalm 9 verse 16

- 2 Peter 1 verse 5–10

- Proverbs 11 verse 2

- Proverbs 11 verse 5

- Proverbs 11 verse 9

- Proverbs 11 verse 16

- Proverbs 11 verse 22

- Proverbs 11 verse 25

- Proverbs 11 verse 30

- 2 Peter 1 verse 1–2

- 2 Peter 1 verse 10–11

- 2 Peter 2 verse 12–17

- 2 Peter 2 verse 19

- 2 Peter 2 verse 21

- Proverbs 12 verse 9

- Proverbs 12 verse 15

- Proverbs 12 verse 24

- Proverbs 12 verse 28

- 2 Peter 3 verse 1–8

- 2 Peter 3 verse 8–9

- 2 Peter 3 verse 10

- 2 Peter 3 verse 16

- Proverbs 13 verse 7

- Proverbs 13 verse 11

- Proverbs 13 verse 12

- Proverbs 13 verse 13

- Proverbs 13 verse 15

- Proverbs 13 verse 18

- Proverbs 13 verse 19

- Proverbs 13 verse 22

- Proverbs 13 verse 23

- Proverbs 13 verse 24

- 1 John 1 verse 6

- 1 John 1 verse 8–9

- Proverbs 14 verse 10

- Proverbs 14 verse 16

- Proverbs 14 verse 29

- 1 John 2 verse 3–6

- 1 John 2 verse 7

- 1 John 2 verse 9

- 1 John 2 verse 15–17

- 1 John verse 23

- Proverbs 15 verse 1

- Proverbs 15 verse 3

- Proverbs 15 verse 5

- Proverbs 15 verse 10

- Proverbs 15 verse 15

- Proverbs 15 verse 33

- 1 John 3 verse 15

- 1 John 3 verse 18

- 1 John 3 verse 21

- Proverbs 16 verse 1

- Proverbs 16 verse 2

- Proverbs 16 verse 9

- Psalm 15

- 1 John 4 verse 1

- 1 John 4 verse 2

- 1 John 4 verse 4

- 1 John 4 verse 18

- Proverbs 17 verse 1

- Proverbs 17 verse 4

- Proverbs 17 verse 5

- Proverbs 17 verse 10

- Proverbs 17 verse 14

- Proverbs 17 verse 15

- Proverbs 17 verse 17

- Proverbs 17 verse 22

- Proverbs 17 verse 28

- Proverbs 18 verse 1

- Proverbs 18 verse 2

- Proverbs 18 verse 21

- Proverbs 18 verse 22

- Proverbs 18 verse 24

- Genesis 16 verse 7

- 2 Chronicles verse 9

- Proverbs 19 verse 14

- 3 John verse 11

- Psalm 18 verse 30

- Proverbs 20 verse 1

- Proverbs 20 verse 3

- Proverbs 20 verse 5

- Proverbs 20 verse 11

- Proverbs 20 verse 13

- Proverbs 20 verse 15

- Proverbs 20 verse 18

- Proverbs 20 verse 22

- Proverbs 20 verse 24

- Proverbs 21 verse 2

- Proverbs 21 verse 3

- Proverbs 21 verse 6

- Proverbs 21 verse 27

- Proverbs 22 verse 6

- Proverbs 22 verse 8

- Proverbs 22 verse 24–25

- Proverbs 23 verse 4

- Proverbs 23 verse 9

- Proverbs 23 verse 13

- Psalm 22

- Proverbs 24 verse 1

- Proverbs 24 verse 10

- Proverbs 24 verse 17–18

- Proverbs 24 verse 23

- Proverbs 24 verse 28

- Proverbs 24 verse 29

- Revelations 3 verse 16

- Revelations 3 verse 20

- Proverbs 25 verse 6

- Proverbs 25 verse 14

- Proverbs 25 verse 15

- Proverbs 25 verse 17

- Proverbs 25 verse 21–22

- Proverbs 25 verse 27

- Proverbs 25 verse 28

- Proverbs 26 verse 5

- Proverbs 26 verse 12

- Proverbs 26 verse 18–19

- Proverbs 27 verse 2

- Proverbs 27 verse 5

- Proverbs 27 verse 6

- Proverbs 27 verse 7

- Proverbs 27 verse 12

- Proverbs 27 verse 14

- Proverbs 28 verse 1

- Proverbs 28 verse 4

- Proverbs 28 verse 5

- Proverbs 28 verse 9

- Proverbs 28 verse 13

- Proverbs 28 verse 20

- Proverbs 29 verse 1

- Proverbs 29 verse 2

- Proverbs 29 verse 11

- Proverbs 29 verse 15

- Proverbs 29 verse 26

- Proverbs 30 verse 5

- Proverbs 30 verse 6

- Proverbs 30 verse 12

- Proverbs 30 verse 21–23

- Proverbs 31 verse 3

- Psalm 30 verse 5

- Isaiah 1 verse 13–17

- Isaiah 1 verse 18

- Isaiah 3 verse 9

- Isaiah 3 verse 10

- Psalm 32 verse 2

- Isaiah 3 verse 9

- Psalm 33 verse 3

- Psalm 33 verse 5

- Psalm 33 verse 10

- Revelations 16 verse 15

- Psalm 34 verse 8

- Psalm 34 verse 9

- Psalm 34 verse 10

- Psalm 34 verse 13

- Psalm 34 verse 22

- Isaiah 5 verse 20

- Psalm 35

- Isaiah 5 verse 13

- Isaiah 5 verse 18

- Psalm 37 verse 1–4

- Psalm 37 verse 8

- Psalm 37 verse 16

- Psalm 37 verse 19

- Psalm 37 verse 23

- Entire Psalm 38

- Isaiah 9 verse 2

- Psalm 32 verse 8–9

- Revelations 21 verse 7

- Entire Psalm 41

- Isaiah 12 verse 1

- Psalm 50 verse 16–23

AUTHOR INFO

Joseph Olabiyi Johnson

Joseph Olabiyi Johnson was born in East London on the 8th of September 1980. A Londoner through and through, Joseph was also very aware of his Nigerian heritage while growing up and has spent about half his life in each country.

From a very early age, he fell in love with the world of sci-fi, fantasy and action adventure, and as young as six years old attempted to create comics. He began writing short stories at the age of twelve because collaborating with his artistically gifted cousin was too frustrating. This in turn gave birth to Joseph's action adventure writing style that on paper screams to be made visual.

A strong martial arts background is also evident in his work for since 1998 Joseph has trained as a martial artist and is currently a Wing Chun instructor in the East London area.

Joseph also has a passion for setting up and co-ordinating community projects that give back to society through youth development. In the last seven years, through various projects with numerous organisations, Joseph has focused the minds of young people through martial arts, led motivational workshops providing career counselling for ethnic minority teenagers, co-ordinated a project dedicated to helping 15-16 year olds outside mainstream education, and has set up a weekend forum that helps people discover their potential.

Unlike his first two novels that are simply a combination of boyhood fantasies and a strong interest in the action adventure genre, 'What do you feel?" is a simple taste of Joseph's beliefs and perspectives. 50% of all royalties made from Joseph's books will be pumped into a youth development organisation set up by him in 2004.

www.josepholabiyijohnson.com

Anthea. Arklie @
Brookstreet. Co. uk

0207

Printed in the United Kingdom
by Lightning Source UK Ltd.
103491UKS00001B/121-213